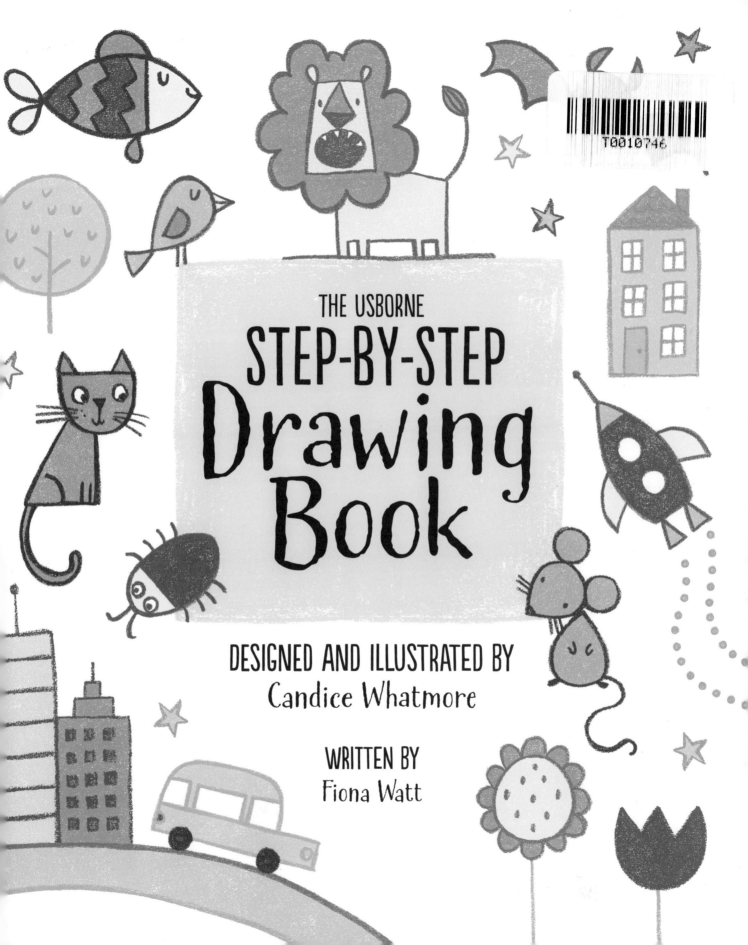

THE USBORNE
STEP-BY-STEP
Drawing
Book

DESIGNED AND ILLUSTRATED BY
Candice Whatmore

WRITTEN BY
Fiona Watt

How to draw a dog

Your turn...

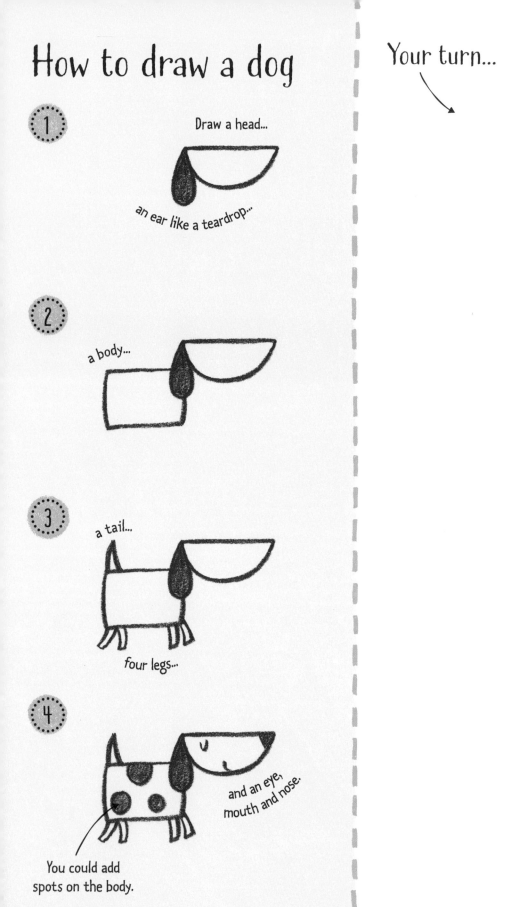

1 Draw a head...

an ear like a teardrop...

2 a body...

3 a tail...

four legs...

4 and an eye, mouth and nose.

You could add spots on the body.

2

Try this... use the same dog's head, but try different body shapes.

a hairy body   a long body   a square body   long legs

How to draw a car

 1

Draw a long rectangle...

 2

a curved roof...

 3

three windows...

 4

two wheels...

 5

a rear light...

front light...

and wheel arches.

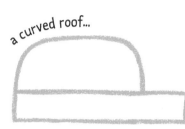

Your turn...

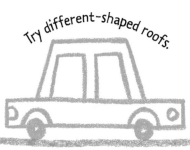

Try different-shaped roofs.

How to draw a rabbit

1 Draw a head...

2 two big ears...

3 a body...

Your turn...

4 a leg... and a foot...

5 two front paws...

6 a face, whiskers... and a tail.

Try this...

Draw the same rabbit head that you drew before, then...

draw a body...

add a back leg and a tail...

and two front paws.

How to draw a cat

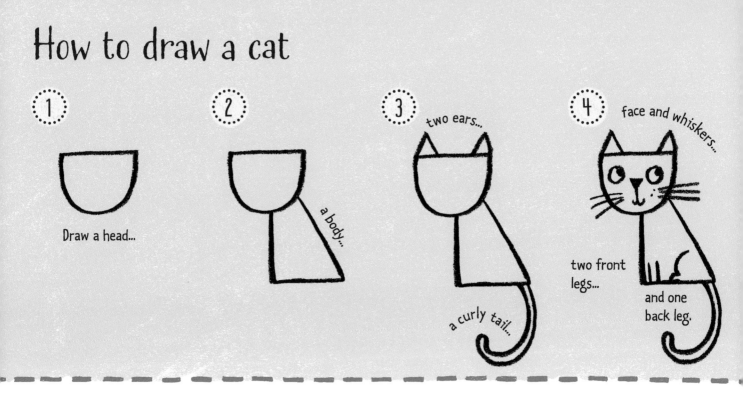

1. Draw a head...

2. a body...

3. two ears...
   a curly tail...

4. face and whiskers...
   two front legs...
   and one back leg.

Your turn...

How to draw trees

1 Draw a teardrop shape...

2 and a trunk and branches.

1 A circle...

2 and a trunk and branches.

1 Draw a shape like this...

2 and a trunk and branches.

1 A cloud shape...

2 and a trunk and branches.

Your turn...

10

Try adding leaves...

or fruit.

How to draw a flower...

1 — Draw a circle...

2 — lots of petals...

3 — lots of dots... a stalk...

4 — and two leaves.

Your turn...

and another.

1   *Draw a 'U' shape...*

a zigzag line...   2

3   a stalk...

4   and two leaves.

Add some flowers to these stalks...

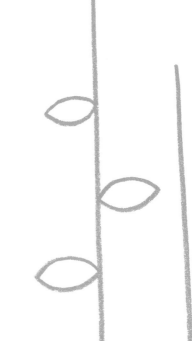

How to draw a mouse

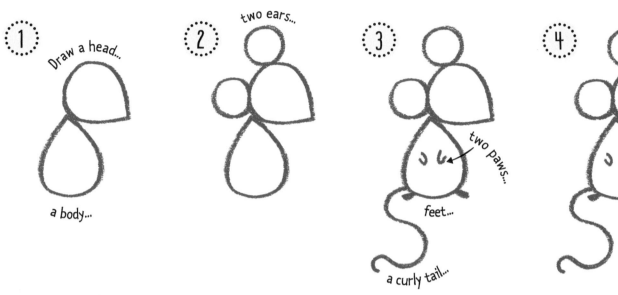

1 Draw a head...

a body...

2 two ears...

3 two paws...

feet...

a curly tail...

4 eyes, a nose...

and whiskers.

Your turn...

How to draw a fish

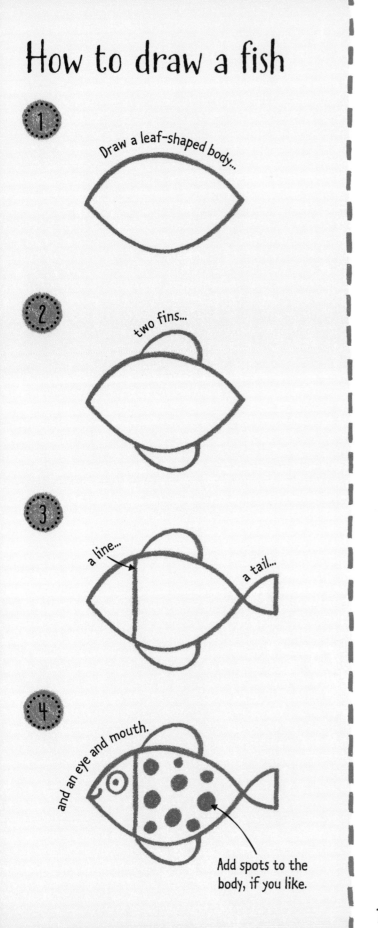

1. Draw a leaf-shaped body...

2. two fins...

3. a line... a tail...

4. and an eye and mouth.

Add spots to the body, if you like.

Your turn...

16

Try this...
you can create lots of different fish by using stripes, zigzags, spots or dots to decorate. You can also try the following...

different-shaped fins   a smaller body   or a longer body

How to draw a city

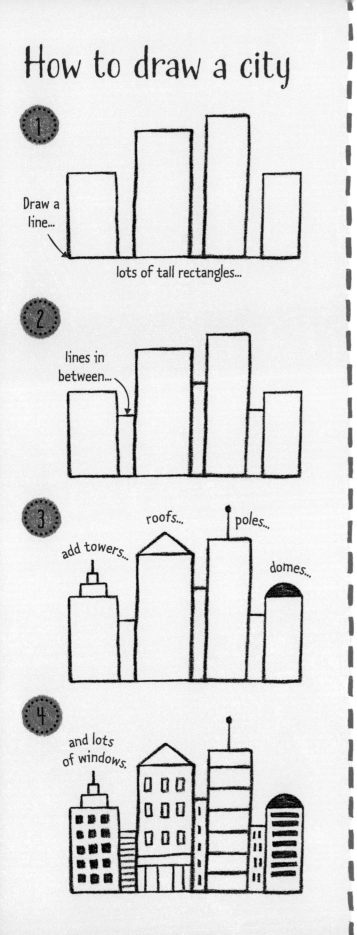

1 Draw a line...

lots of tall rectangles...

2 lines in between...

3 add towers... roofs... poles... domes...

4 and lots of windows.

Your turn...

How to draw a house

Your turn...

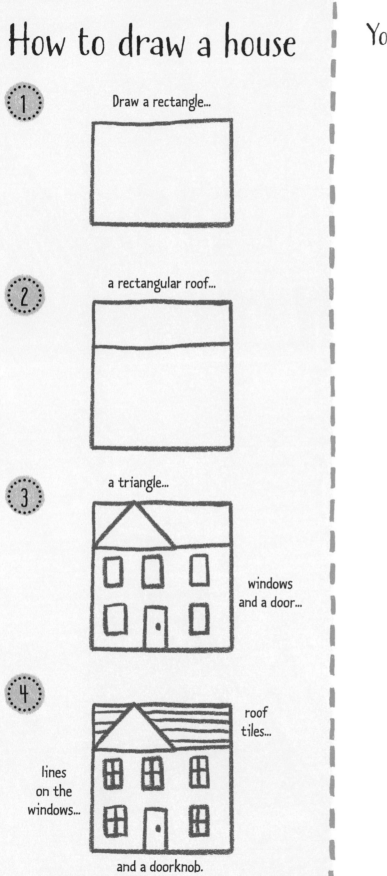

1 Draw a rectangle...

2 a rectangular roof...

3 a triangle... windows and a door...

4 roof tiles... lines on the windows... and a doorknob.

Try this... create different houses by just changing a few things. How about...

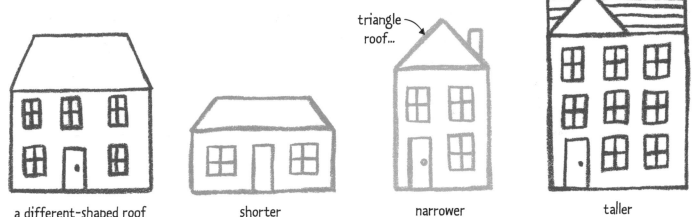

a different-shaped roof   shorter   triangle roof...   narrower   taller

How to draw a horse

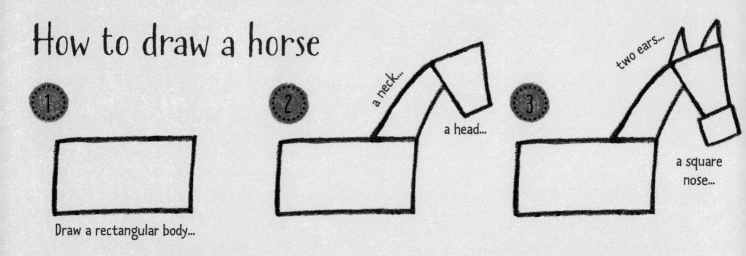

1 Draw a rectangular body...

2 a neck... a head...

3 two ears... a square nose...

Your turn...

4 four legs...

5 a tail...

a zigzag mane...

eyes...

and two nostrils.

You could draw shapes like these for grass.

How to draw a bird

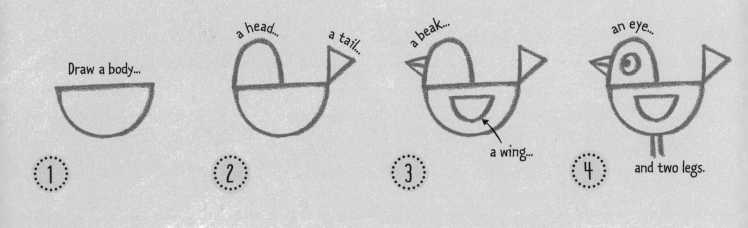

Draw a body... a head... a tail... a beak... a wing... an eye... and two legs.

① ② ③ ④

Your turn...

Try drawing different tails, beaks, eyes and wings.

How to draw an owl

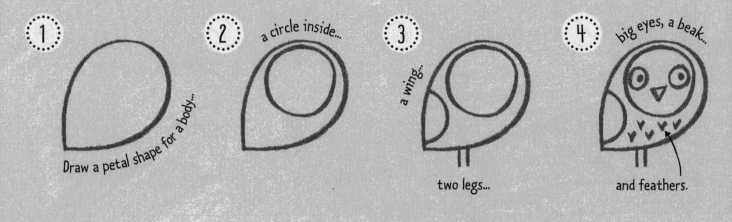

1 Draw a petal shape for a body...

2 a circle inside...

3 a wing... two legs...

4 big eyes, a beak... and feathers.

Your turn...

How to draw a knight

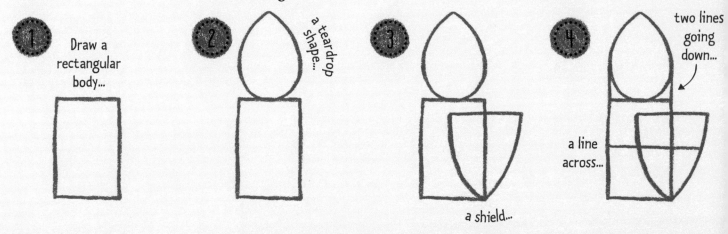

1 Draw a rectangular body...

2 a teardrop shape...

3 a shield...

4 two lines going down... a line across...

Your turn...

5

a line...

an arm...

legs and feet...

6

a sword...

a line for a helmet...

a hand...

7

eyes and a mouth...

and a dashed line.

Fill in the suit.

Try this...

Make your knight look different by...

using stripes instead of shading

drawing a full-face helmet

changing the shape of the shield

29

How to draw a castle

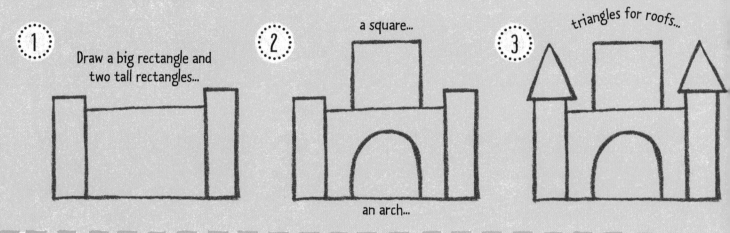

1 Draw a big rectangle and two tall rectangles...

2 a square... an arch...

3 triangles for roofs...

Your turn...

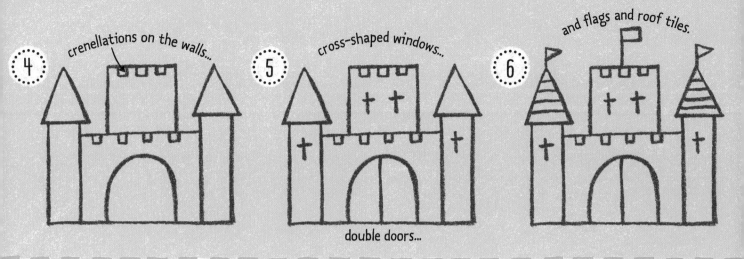

4 crenellations on the walls...

5 cross-shaped windows...

double doors...

6 and flags and roof tiles.

How to draw a princess

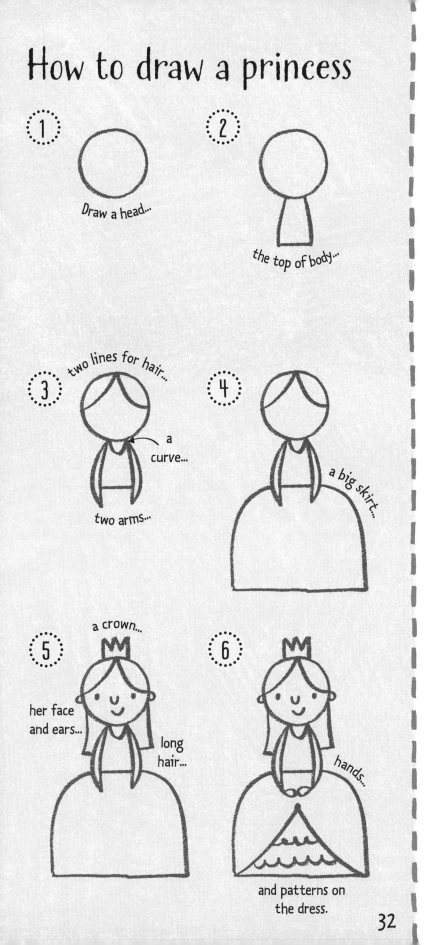

1. Draw a head...

2. the top of body...

3. two lines for hair... a curve... two arms...

4. a big skirt...

5. a crown... her face and ears... long hair...

6. hands... and patterns on the dress.

Your turn...

32

How to draw a dragon

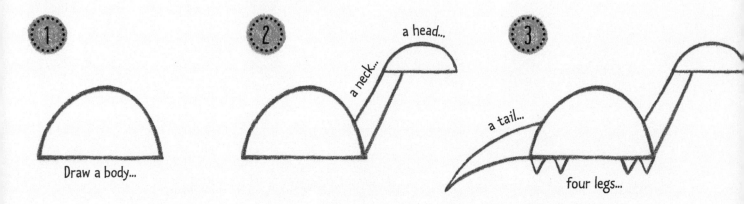

1 Draw a body...

2 a neck... a head...

3 a tail... four legs...

Your turn...

How to draw a bat

Your turn...

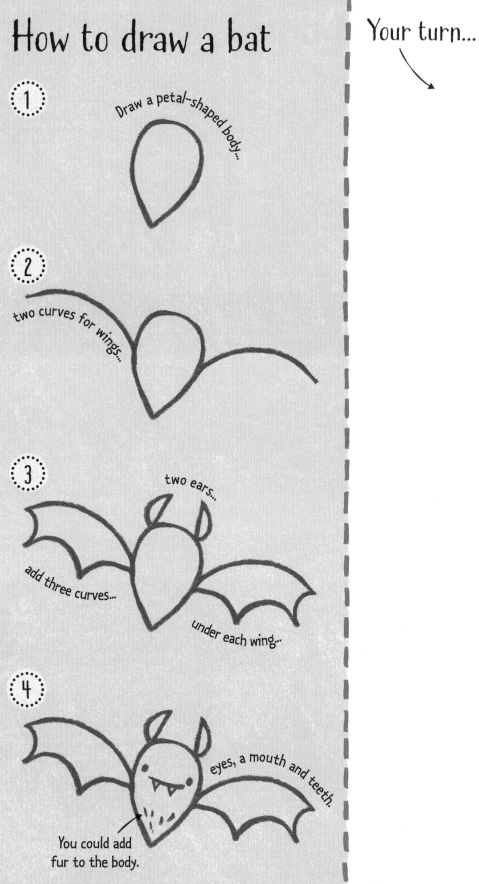

1 Draw a petal-shaped body...

2 two curves for wings...

3 two ears...
add three curves...
under each wing...

4 eyes, a mouth and teeth.
You could add fur to the body.

36

Add stars...

to decorate a
bat scene.

How to draw bugs

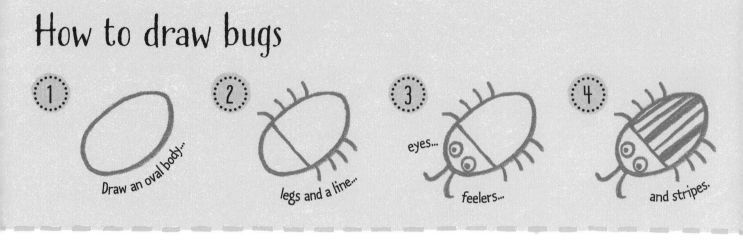

1 Draw an oval body...

2 legs and a line...

3 eyes... feelers...

4 and stripes.

Your turn...

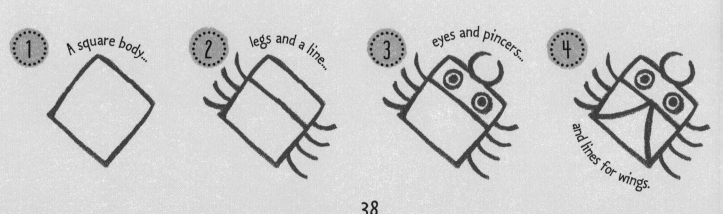

1 A square body...

2 legs and a line...

3 eyes and pincers...

4 and lines for wings.

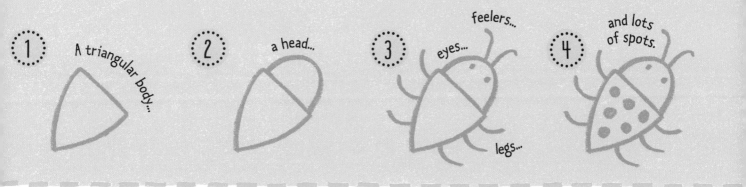

1 A triangular body...

2 a head...

3 feelers... eyes... legs...

4 and lots of spots.

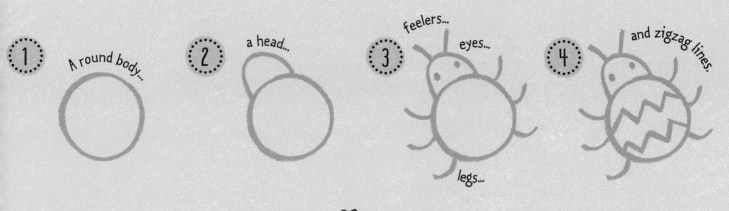

1 A round body...

2 a head...

3 feelers... eyes... legs...

4 and zigzag lines.

How to draw a robot

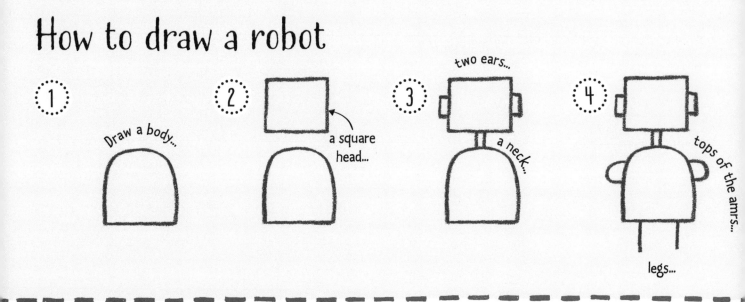

① Draw a body...

② a square head...

③ two ears... a neck...

④ tops of the amrs... legs...

Your turn...

(5) **a face panel...**
arms and hands...
feet...

(6) **eyes and a mouth...**
a tummy and buttons...

(7) **and an antenna.**
Fill in the face panel.

Try this...

Draw different shaped bodies for your robot. You could use wheels instead of legs too. Here are some ideas. You could copy these or invent your own.

41

How to draw a mad scientist

1 Draw a head...

2 a body...

3 big messy hair...

Your turn...

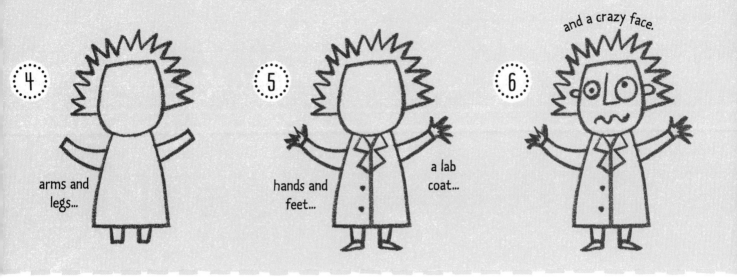

4 arms and legs...

5 hands and feet... a lab coat...

6 and a crazy face.

How to draw a monster

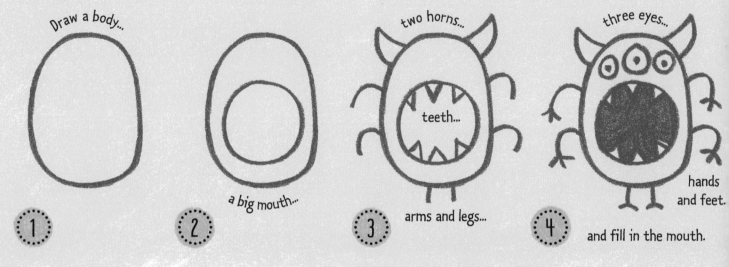

Draw a body...

a big mouth...

two horns...

teeth...

arms and legs...

three eyes...

hands and feet.

and fill in the mouth.

1 2 3 4

Your turn...

How to draw a penguin

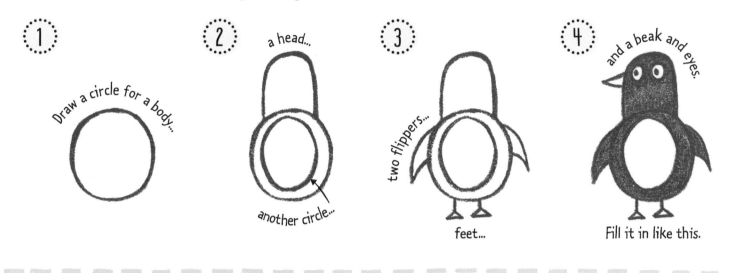

① Draw a circle for a body...

② a head...
another circle...

③ two flippers...
feet...

④ and a beak and eyes.
Fill it in like this.

Your turn...

How to draw a racetrack driver

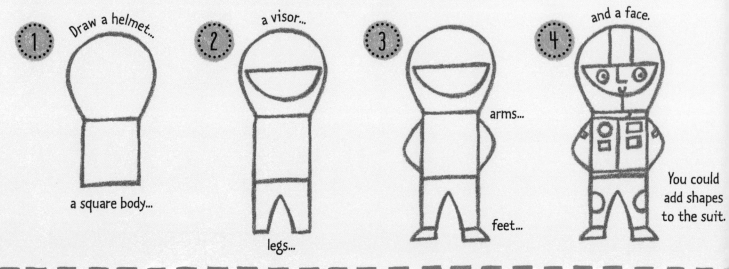

1. Draw a helmet...

a square body...

2. a visor...

legs...

3. arms...

feet...

4. and a face.

You could add shapes to the suit.

Your turn...

Turn over to find out
how to draw his car...

...and a racetrack car

Your turn...

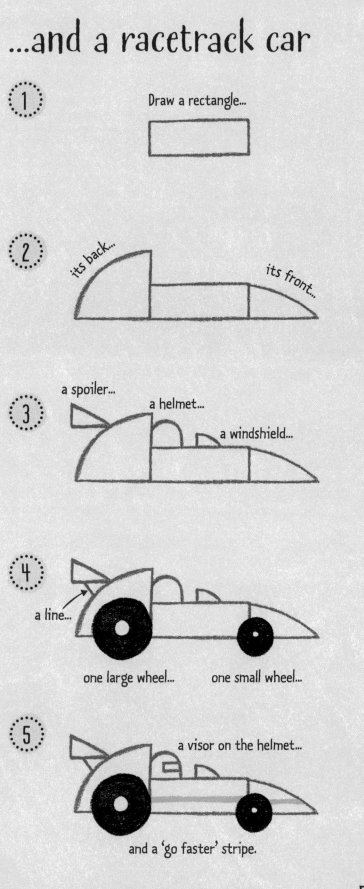

1 Draw a rectangle...

2 its back... its front...

3 a spoiler... a helmet... a windshield...

4 a line... one large wheel... one small wheel...

5 a visor on the helmet... and a 'go faster' stripe.

How to draw a lion

Draw a head with ears...

a curly mane...

a body...

1   2   3

Your turn...

a nose, a mouth...

a tail...

4

the end
of the tail...

teeth...

5

6

and add legs.

A lioness doesn't have a mane.

How to draw an elephant

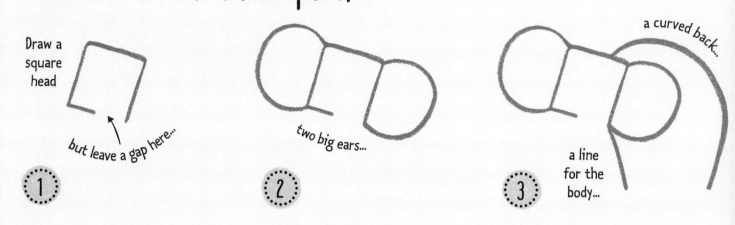

Draw a
square
head

but leave a gap here...

two big ears...

a curved back...

a line
for the
body...

1

2

3

Your turn...

You could try drawing the trunk like this.

4 four legs...

5 a trunk...

6 a face, mouth... and a tail. Add lines on the trunk, too.

How to draw a tiger

1 Draw a square head...

and a body...

2 two ears...

a long tail...

3 a face...

two front legs...

4 and cover with stripes

Your turn...

How to draw a crocodile

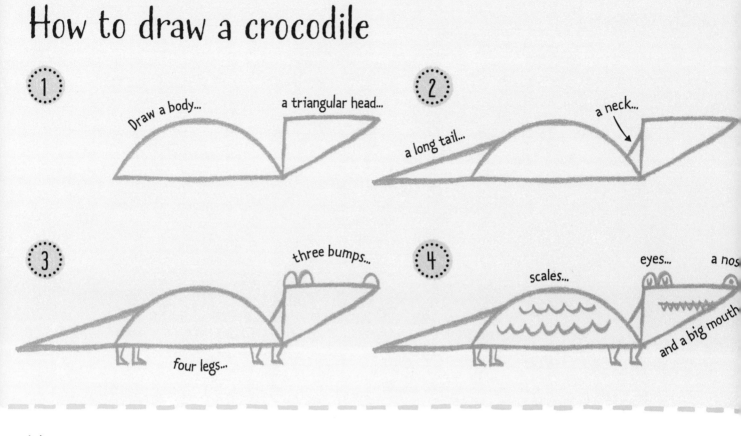

1 Draw a body... a triangular head...

2 a long tail... a neck...

3 three bumps... four legs...

4 scales... eyes... a nos... and a big mouth

Your turn...

Try this...

For a crocodile swimming in water – don't bother to draw the feet. Just draw wavy lines for water.

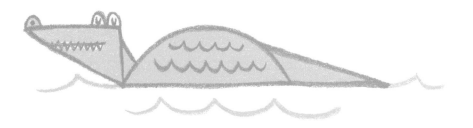

How to draw a monkey

1 Draw a head...

2 then this shape inside...

3 add a body...

Your turn...

two ears...

a curly tail...

a back leg..."

4

5

two front legs...

6

then add the face.

Try this...

Draw the same head that you drew before, then...

add two long arms...

a curly tail...

a body...

and two legs.

How to draw a pirate ship

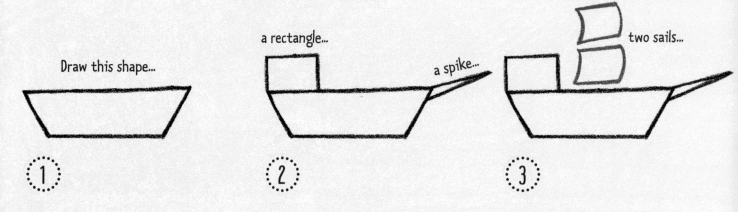

Draw this shape...

a rectangle...

a spike...

two sails...

① ② ③

Your turn...

two more sails...

lines for the masts...

flags...

portholes...

and waves.

4

5

6

How to draw a pirate

1 Draw a head...

2 a line... a beard...

3 a body...

4 arms... legs...

Your turn...

64

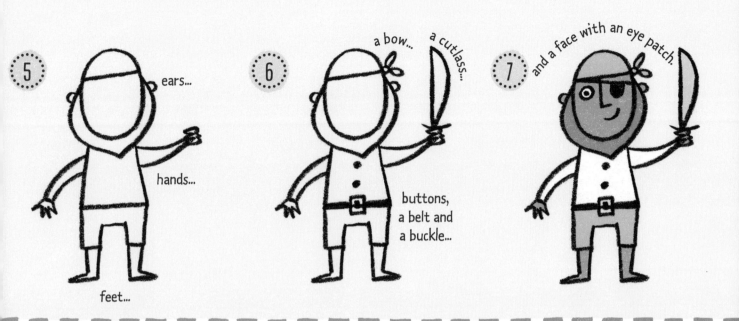

5 ears...

hands...

feet...

6 a bow...   a cutlass...

buttons,
a belt and
a buckle...

7 and a face with an eye patch.

How to draw a shark

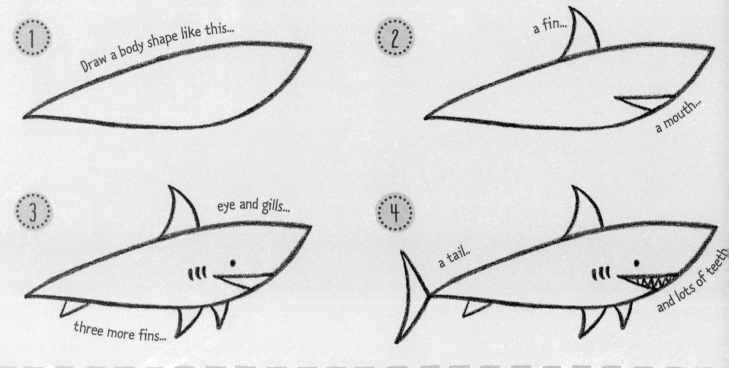

1 Draw a body shape like this...

2 a fin... a mouth...

3 eye and gills... three more fins...

4 a tail.. and lots of teeth

Your turn...

How to draw an octopus

1 Draw a head...

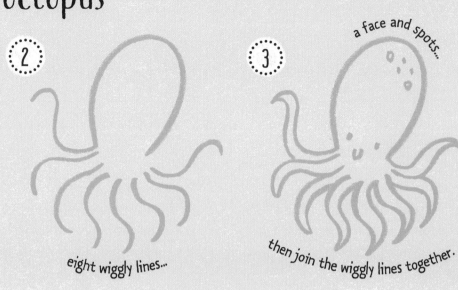

2 eight wiggly lines...

3 a face and spots...

then join the wiggly lines together.

Your turn...

How to draw a panda

Draw a head...

1

a round body...

2

and four legs.

3

Your turn...

Add two ears...

panda eyes...

④

two lines across the body...

⑤

and a nose and mouth.

⑥

Use black to fill in the shapes.

Try this...

For a panda standing up, either copy this one or follow the steps for the bear on the next page, but don't add the long nose when you get to step 5. Instead...

fill in the ears...

add a panda face...

fill the front legs...

then the back legs.

How to draw a bear

Draw a circle...

a round body...

two arms...

Your turn...

4 — two legs...

5 — two ears... a teardrop muzzle...

6 — eyes, a nose, a mouth... and a furry tummy.

Try this...

Follow the steps on the previous two pages to draw a bear on all fours. When you get to step 4, don't draw the panda eyes, but draw these instead...

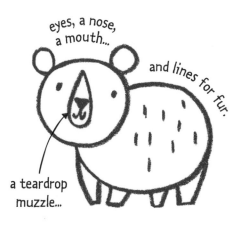

eyes, a nose, a mouth...

and lines for fur.

a teardrop muzzle...

How to draw an alien

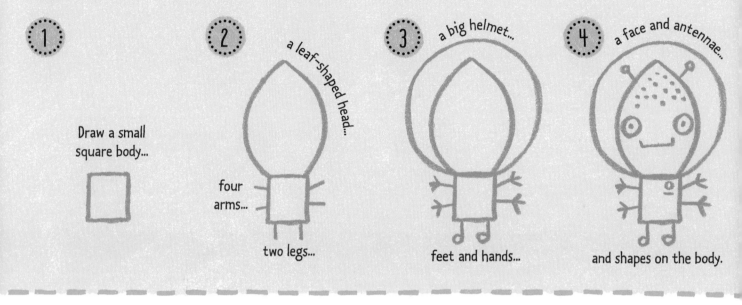

1 Draw a small square body...

2 a leaf-shaped head...

four arms...

two legs...

3 a big helmet...

feet and hands...

4 a face and antennae...

and shapes on the body.

Your turn...

Try an alien in a spaceship. It doesn't need a helmet.

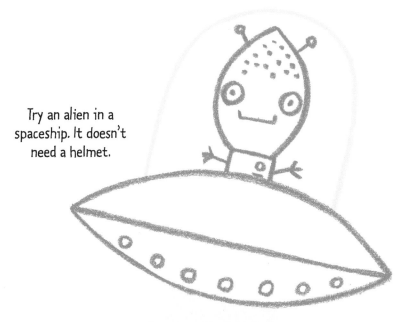

How to draw a rocket

Your turn...

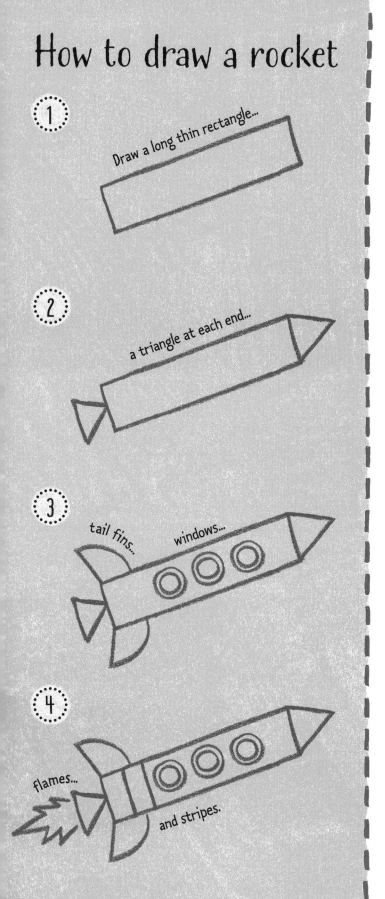

1. Draw a long thin rectangle...

2. a triangle at each end...

3. tail fins... windows...

4. flames... and stripes.

You could vary the
shape of a rocket.

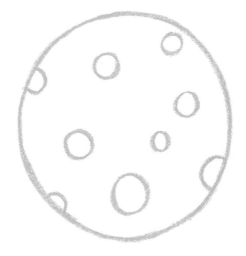

How to draw an astronaut

 1 Draw a circle and an oval inside...

2 a body...

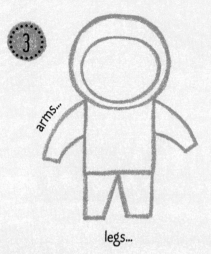

3 arms...

legs...

Your turn...

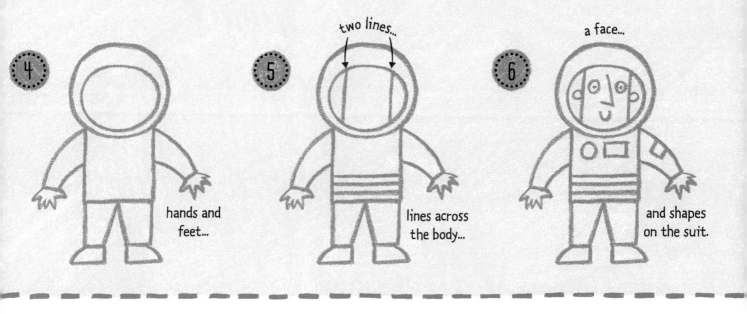

4 hands and feet...

5 two lines... lines across the body...

6 a face... and shapes on the suit.

How to draw a spider

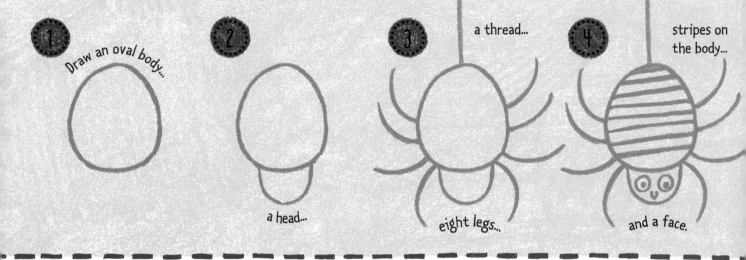

1 Draw an oval body...

2 a head...

3 a thread... eight legs...

4 stripes on the body... and a face.

Your turn...

...and a web.

 Draw lots of lines like this...

starting near the middle, add a small line...

Continue adding lines until it looks like this.

keep adding lines in a spiral shape.

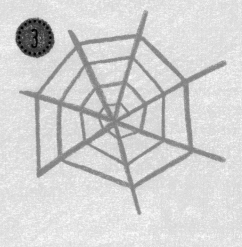

How to draw a lizard

Your turn...

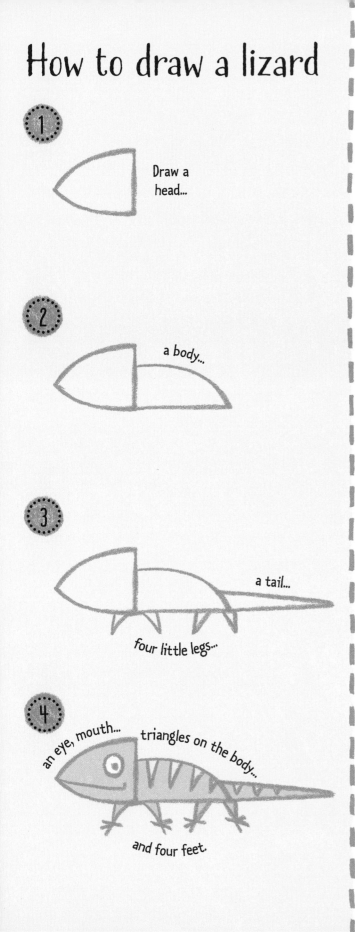

1 Draw a head...

2 a body...

3 a tail...

four little legs...

4 an eye, mouth... triangles on the body...

and four feet.

How to draw a frog

1 Draw a big number eight...

2 two back legs and feet...

3 two front legs and feet...

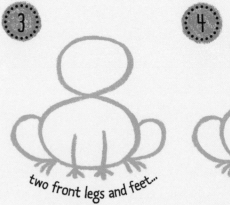

4 eyes... and a mouth.

Your turn...

You could add a lily pad.

How to draw a snake

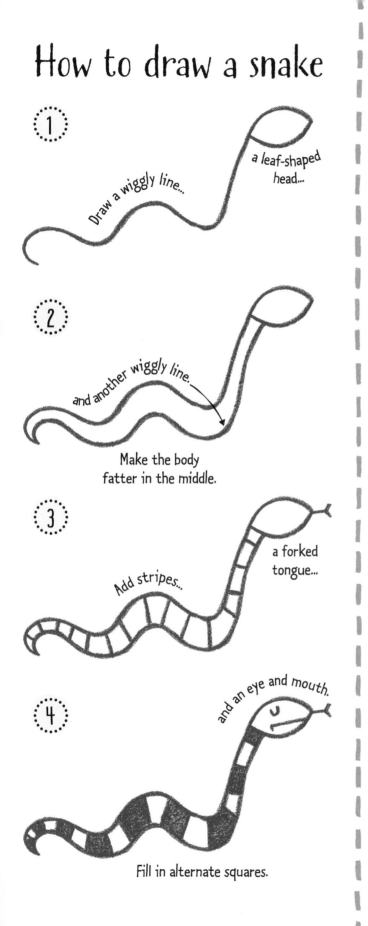

1
Draw a wiggly line...
a leaf-shaped head...

2
and another wiggly line.
Make the body fatter in the middle.

3
Add stripes...
a forked tongue...

4
and an eye and mouth.
Fill in alternate squares.

Your turn...

How to draw faces

smiley surprised happy sad angry

tired excited upset asleep content

Your turn... Draw different expressions on these heads, then draw some of your own...

Add hair...

shaved   curly   straight   long   short   pigtails

and accessories

glasses   eyebrows   beard   winter hat   cowboy hat   straw hat

How to draw animal heads

koala   squirrel   seal   puppy   chicken   pig

Your turn... Draw circles and then copy some of these simple faces...

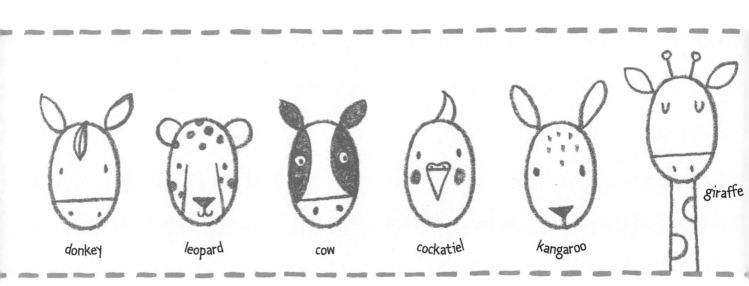

donkey   leopard   cow   cockatiel   kangaroo   giraffe

Your turn... Draw ovals and then try these faces...

fox   raccoon   deer   dog   bison

snake   cat   goat   walrus   rhino

Your turn... Draw faces on these shapes, then try some more of your own...

Create a scene

The following pages have ideas for scenes created from pictures in the book. Finish off the pictures, then use the ideas to create some of your own.

Add more trees.

Draw more horses in the field.

Add more rabbits.

Draw flowers in the meadow.

Draw a city on
the hill.

Add more cars.

Draw birds in
the tree...

and bugs on leaves.

93

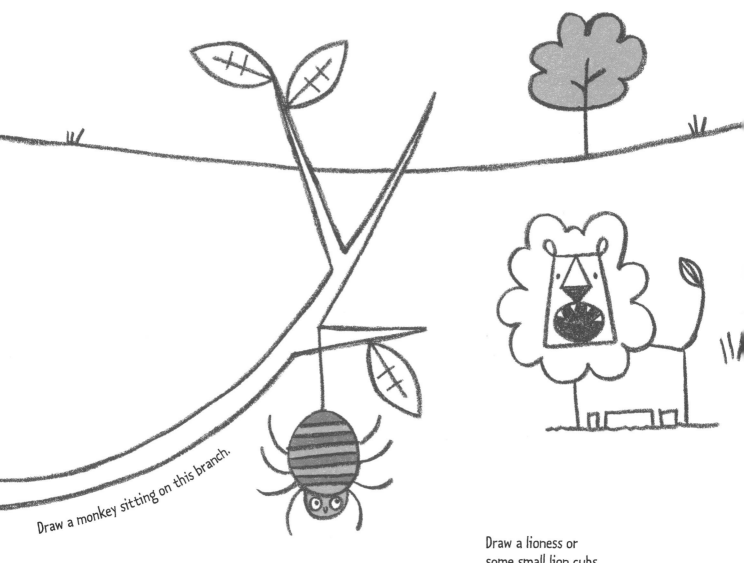

Draw a monkey sitting on this branch.

Draw a lioness or
some small lion cubs.

Add a spider's web.

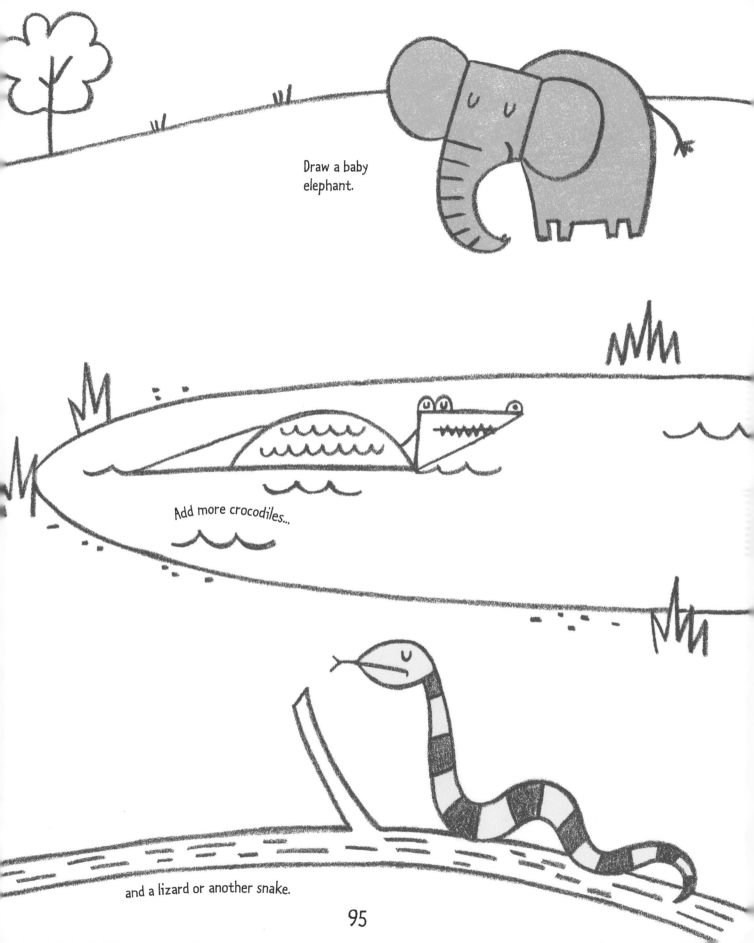

Draw a baby elephant.

Add more crocodiles...

and a lizard or another snake.

Draw more planets.

Add stars in the sky.

Add more rockets or alien spacecraft.

Add an alien or another astronaut.

With thanks to Keith Furnival

First published in 2014 by Usborne Publishing Limited, 83-85 Saffron Hill, London EC1N 8RT, England.
usborne.com © 2014 Usborne Publishing Limited. The name Usborne and the Balloon logo are Trade Marks of Usborne Publishing Limited.